Language Builders

Andrew and Allen Learn about
ADVERBS

by Joanna Jarc Robinson
illustrated by Robin Boyer

Content Consultant
Roxanne Owens
Associate Professor, Elementary Reading
DePaul University

NORWOOD HOUSE ▦ PRESS
CHICAGO, ILLINOIS

Norwood House Press
P.O. Box 316598
Chicago, Illinois 60631
For information regarding Norwood House Press, please visit
our website at:
www.norwoodhousepress.com or call 866-565-2900.

Editor: Melissa York
Designer: Jake Nordby
Project Management: Red Line Editorial

Paperback ISBN: 978-1-60357-704-5

The Library of Congress has cataloged the original hardcover
edition with the following call number: 2014030262

Manufactured in the United States of America in North
Mankato, Minnesota.
262N—122014

Words in **black bold** are defined in the glossary.

Taking Notes Creatively

Just call me Andrew, Zoologist, Observer, and Field Note-Taker Extraordinaire. I may not have a lot of practice yet, but I will be an expert after tomorrow's field trip. We are visiting the zoo, and we get to see the new Arctic Animal Exhibit, too. Our science teacher, Mr. Hammond, wants us to practice observing nature. We will record what we see just like real scientists do.

Mr. Hammond wants us to write with lots of **adverbs**. These words describe where, when, and how the animals move, eat, sleep, play, and interact with other animals. According to Mr. Hammond, many adverbs end in –ly, so I guess I will be writing creatively, specifically, thoughtfully, legibly, and, of course, scientifically. Tomorrow should be very interesting.

By Andrew, age 9

"Listen up, everybody," Mr. Hammond called from the front of the bus. "Does everyone have a journal for taking field notes?"

The class answered, "Yes!"

"Today, you will observe the animals. You will record your observations in your journal. That is what real scientists do. You must use complete sentences. You should also use several adverbs. Does anyone remember what an adverb is?"

Nobody answered. Mr. Hammond continued, "An adverb describes an action or a verb. Adverbs answer questions about how, where, or when something happens."

Andrew raised his hand, "I thought an **adjective** was a describing word."

"That's true," said Mr. Hammond, "but an adjective describes a noun, a person, place, or thing. If you described an elephant, what might you say?"

Allen said, "Huge, gray, fat, wrinkly." Everyone giggled.

"Exactly. Those are adjectives," said Mr. Hammond. "Now, imagine you want to describe how an elephant moves. What might you say?"

Allen looked confused. Lily answered, "It moves slowly."

"Good," said Mr. Hammond, "*Slowly* is an adverb. What about where and when an elephant eats?"

Andrew joked, "Wherever and whenever he wants!" Everyone giggled again. "Right," said Mr. Hammond. "*Wherever* and *whenever* are adverbs!"

"I thought adverbs usually ended in *–ly,*" said Peg.

Mr. Hammond explained, "Many adverbs are spelled like the related adjective with *–ly* added, but not all of them. Identifying adverbs is all about seeing how the words work in the sentence. If a word tells how, when, or where an action happens, it is probably an adverb."

Soon the bus arrived at the zoo. Mr. Hammond reminded the class, "Please write your notes thoughtfully, specifically, and legibly."

"Hey! Those are adverbs!" shouted Andrew.

Mr. Hammond knew the children were ready to take field notes.

First, the class visited the zoo's two lions. The lion walked out from inside the house. He woke up the lioness. The lioness roared. Then she swatted at him with her paw. He turned around quickly. He walked back into the house.

"Wow. She means business," said Andrew. "Do not mess with the lioness!"

He wrote in his journal:

The lioness roared at the lion.

Allen noticed something. "I don't see any adverbs in your sentence. That just tells what the lioness did. You have to write how the lioness roared."

AFRICAN LION

11

Andrew wrote:

The lioness roared <u>loudly</u> at the lion.

Allen wrote:

The lion <u>suddenly</u> bothered the lioness. She was sleeping <u>quietly</u>. She smacked him <u>hard</u> with her paw. He disappeared <u>quickly</u> back inside the house.

"Wow! You have lots of adverbs in that field note! I need to start writing more intelligently," said Andrew. He sensed there was a friendly adverb competition brewing.

Allen rolled his eyes. Andrew secretly wrote himself an adverb reminder at the top of a clean page.

How? When? Where?

Next, the class stopped by the black bear exhibit. "Check out that sleeping bear!" Andrew said, pointing to the black bear slumped over a huge rock.

Andrew thought for a second. He wrote:

The <u>very</u> tired bear slept <u>peacefully</u> and <u>comfortably</u>.

Allen read the sentence. "Did you know *very* is an adverb too? Adverbs can also modify adjectives, or change their meaning. The bear isn't just tired, it's *very* tired."

"Right," agreed Andrew. "And adverbs can also modify other adverbs."

He wrote:

The bear slept <u>so peacefully</u>.

Next, Allen and Andrew watched the giraffe. She stretched her neck up high. She grabbed some leaves with her big, dark tongue. She lowered her neck. She gave the leaves to her baby. Allen started to write, "The mother giraffe stretched . . ." He paused to think about *how* she stretched.

"I know," said Andrew. "She stretched gracefully."

"That's a good one," said Allen.

Allen wrote:

The mother giraffe stretched <u>gracefully</u>.

"Hey! You stole my adverb. Now I have to think of another one," said Andrew.

Andrew wrote:

The baby giraffe waited <u>hungrily</u> for the leaves.

"'Hungrily' is spelled a little differently," noticed Allen.

"Yes," agreed Andrew. "Sometimes you can't just add *–ly* to an adjective, like when the adjective already ends with *–y*, usually. So the adjective is hungry, and the adverb is *hungrily.*"

"If the adjective ends with *–e*, you usually drop it, too," added Allen. "Like incredible, *incredibly.*"

"But not polite, *politely*!" crowed Andrew. "That's one exception to the rule."

"This is getting complicated," said Allen with a smile. "I'll have to use a dictionary if I'm not sure how to spell something."

Finally, the class reached the new Arctic Animal Exhibit. Mr. Hammond asked the class to focus on adverbs that answer questions about where or when. Still, Allen was not sure what to write. Andrew read the sign about polar bears. He asked, "Did you know that polar bear mothers often give birth to twins?"

Just then, two small polar bear cubs came out from the back of the exhibit. They splashed noisily into the pool and swam up to their mother, who was swimming by the glass at the front of the exhibit.

"Look," said Andrew. "One is swimming faster than the other."

"*Faster* is a **comparative adverb**," agreed Allen. "A comparative adverb compares two actions."

"I bet the mother can swim fastest of all," said Andrew. "And fastest is a **superlative adverb**! It compares more than two actions. Fast, faster, fastest!"

"Next up—sea lions!" Mr. Hammond said. "Please try to include a note about *how often* sea lions do an action."

The sea lions were just about to eat. The zookeeper told the children that sea lions eat fish three times daily. They bark enthusiastically when they are hungry.

Andrew wrote:

The sea lions swim <u>gracefully</u>. They <u>often</u> bark <u>enthusiastically</u>. The sea lions eat <u>frequently</u>, three times a day. They <u>always</u> eat fish.

Andrew proudly showed Allen his notes.

"I wonder if they eat more frequently than the polar bears," said Allen.

"I don't know," said Andrew. "But I know that's another comparative adverb. Frequently, *more frequently*."

"And *most frequently* is the superlative," added Allen. "We add *more* and *most* to many adverbs rather than changing the endings."

"Or *less* and *least*," agreed Andrew. "Is it lunchtime yet? We're eating less frequently than the sea lions!"

Allen laughed as the two walked out of the Arctic Animal Exhibit.

"Last stop, the monkey house," announced Mr. Hammond. Andrew and Allen loved the monkeys. They also really loved imitating the monkeys.

First, one of the monkeys hooted loudly at the boys. "I can top that!" said Andrew, and he hooted more loudly at the monkey.

"Listen to this!" said Allen, and he hooted the most loudly of all.

Then the monkey scratched his armpits. Andrew and Allen scratched very vigorously. Everyone watched eagerly. They wanted to see what the monkey would do next.

Finally, the monkey stuck out his tongue at Andrew and Allen. They laughed hysterically! Then they stuck out their tongues at the monkey.

The monkey did not seem to like that. He pounded loudly and powerfully on the glass. Yikes! Andrew and Allen backed away nervously. The rest of the class thought it was ridiculously funny!

Andrew started taking notes from a safe distance.

The monkey has curly hair.

Allen stopped him. "Curly is an adjective," he said. "Not all words that end in –ly are adverbs. You have to pay attention to how the word works in the sentence."

"Thanks!" said Andrew. "I'll watch out!"

The class got back onto the bus. Mr. Hammond asked the class to review their notes on the way home. He suggested they add a few drawings. He said he would collect the journals back at school.

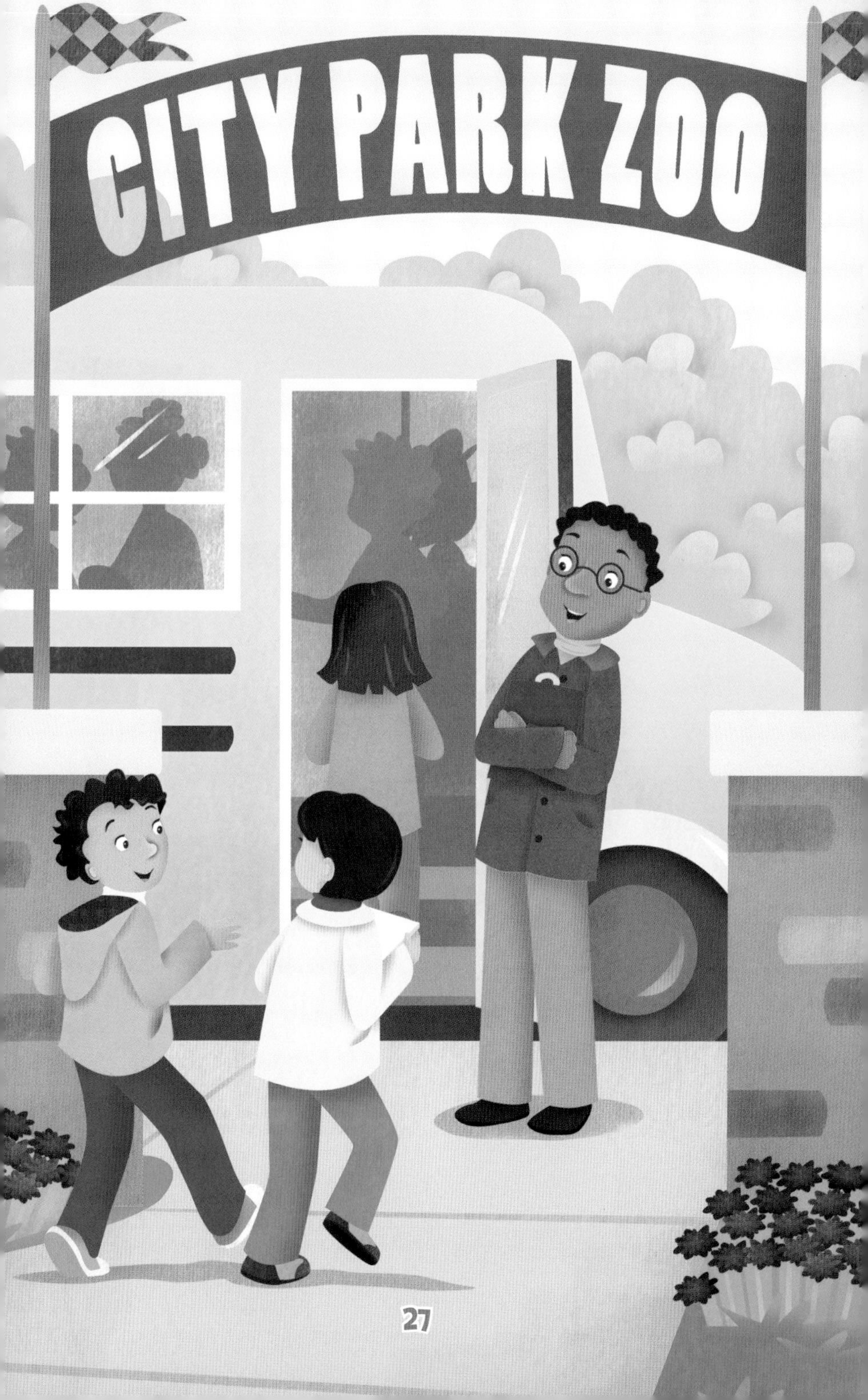
CITY PARK ZOO

Andrew and Allen slowly paged through their journals. Andrew sketched the monkey. The monkey's tongue was sticking out. Allen laughed so hard he couldn't hold his pencil straight.

Finally, the bus arrived at school. The children got off the bus. Mr. Hammond collected the journals.

"I feel like a real scientist," said Andrew. "Writing field notes isn't so hard, once you get the hang of it."

"Yeah," said Allen. "Writing adverbs isn't so hard either. Especially if your friend helps you write clearly, cheerfully, and terrifically!"

The two laughed loudly and headed back to the classroom.

Adverbs describe where, when, and how the action in a sentence happens. A sentence doesn't need adverbs, but adverbs can make your writing more specific and more interesting. The zebra doesn't just gallop; it gallops *gracefully*. The lion doesn't just yawn; it yawns *enormously*.

Many words that end in *–ly* are adverbs. But not all words that end in *–ly* are adverbs, and not all adverbs end in *–ly*. The only way to spot an adverb for sure is to see how it works in the sentence. If a word tells how, when, or where an action happens, it is probably an adverb.

One adverb can modify another adverb: The tortoise ate *extremely slowly*. An adverb can also modify an adjective: The bird's feathers were *very* red. Comparative and superlative adverbs compare more than one action. One monkey jumped *quickly*, another jumped *more quickly*, but the third jumped the *most quickly* of all. Comparative and superlative adverbs often have the words *more*, *most*, *less*, or *least*.

Read the text on page 25 again. How many adverbs can you find there? Some sentences have more than one adverb. Can you find the comparative and superlative adverbs?

Writing Activity

1. Find a notebook or staple together some sheets of paper to record your thoughts and observations. Write your name and a title for your field notes on the cover.

2. On the first page, write HOW? On the second page, write WHEN? On the third page, write WHERE?

3. Choose an animal or a human subject to observe. Watch HOW he or she acts. How does your subject move? How does your subject eat? Write a sentence that describes HOW your subject does something.

4. Do the same thing for the other questions. Observe and think about WHEN your subject does an action. Watch WHERE your subject shows an action. When does your subject bark or meow? How often does your subject eat or lick its paws? Where does your subject sit or rest? Write down what you saw using your best descriptive adverbs. You can draw pictures, too!

Glossary

adjective: a word that describes a noun or pronoun.

adverbs: words that describe an action or verb.

comparative adverb: an adverb that compares two things.

superlative adverb: an adverb that compares more than two things.

For More Information

Books

Riggs, Kate. *Grammar Basics: Adverbs*. Mankato, MN: Creative, 2013.

Walton, Rick. *Suddenly Alligator: Adventures in Adverbs*. Layton, UT: Gibbs Smith, 2011.

Websites

Adverb Millions
http://www.quia.com/rr/62022.html
Take this quiz to practice spotting the adverbs in sentences.

Pick It: Adverbs
http://www.ezschool.com/Games/English/Adverbs/Adverbs.html
In this online game, practice selecting the adverb in each sentence.

About the Author

Joanna Jarc Robinson is a funny, quirky, creative children's author, illustrator, and education professional, specializing in Pre-K–8 educational content.